SUCCESS IS THE BEST REVENGE

KIRAN M

DEDICATED TO ALL THOSE PEOPLE

WHO CHANGE THE LIVES OF OTHERS

BY LIVING AS AN EXAMPLE

AND

BY EMPOWERING OTHERS FOR GREATNESS.

THANK YOU,

HAVE YOU EMPOWERED SOMEBODY FOR ABSOLUTE GREATNESS TODAY?

Contents

Contents

Contents

Contents

Acknowledgements

Firstly, I would like to thank each and every one for giving me this beautiful opportunity to be as author this book.

A big thank - you to my family, tutors and my friends for mentally supporting me always. I'll always be grateful to them for letting me write my own book.

My hearty thank - you to my team for staying strong beside me when I was working for this book.

Another thank - you for the well-wishers of this book.

Grateful to all the readers embracing the book and making it their own!

Disclaimer

This book has been published with all efforts taken to make the material error-free after the consent of the writer. However, the authors and the publisher do not assume and hereby disclaim any liability to any party for any loss, damage, or disruption caused by errors or omissions, whether such errors or omissions result from negligence, accident, or any other cause. While every effort has been made to avoid any mistake or omission, this publication is being sold on the condition and understanding that neither the Author nor the publishers or printers would be liable in any manner or for any person by reason of any mistake or omission in this publication or for any action taken or omitted to be taken or advice rendered or accepted on the basis of the work. We as Spot write Publications, hold no responsibility to hurt any religious sentiments or political views, with understanding of respective writer.

About Author

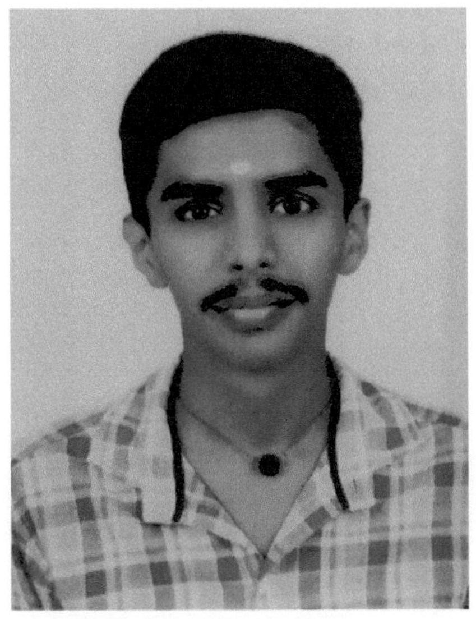

Kiran M HDCA, ADCA, DCN, B.Com(PA)

Kiran is an young energetic and motivational writer and entrepreneur. His nativity is belongs to Kerala. He completed his schoolings at Sri Sowdeswarri Model Matriculation Higher Secondary School with first class. He done his graduation at KG College of Arts and Science, Coimbatore. He started his writing career at the age of 15. He co-authrized for more than 75 books. He authorized for 2 published books. He works on 3 World Record Project and 2 International Record Projects. He writes more than 200 motivational poems and 50+ articles.

He is nominated as nominee of Best Author Award for 4 times and Reader Choice Award for 2 times. He is not only a writer, he is also a blogger. He is running one academic publication Pages Could Talk, one Academics Publication AK Research Consultancy, Freelancing Start-up and he is running his own Tax Consultancy Tax On Tracks. He is MSME certified GST Practitioner.

1. Life Is Not A Race

Life should never be a race,
it's a book with a beautiful pen.
A one in a million triumph,
an overcoming victory in the end.
Life is too short, love with passion,
trust at your own speed,
be loyal to ones who love you, laugh so hard until you pee!
Life is full of music,
some happy, sad, and some with ease.
Dance and sing through unknown
doorways to every beat of life's melodies.
Life is not a race,
its a test with no grade. Live with peace,
love the most,
with the memories you made.

2. Value Of Education

For some it is a privilege
For others it's a right
The difference between darkness
And a future that is bright.
Some will think a burden
Where others see a gift
The key to moving forward
And to give your life a lift.
If school is not your calling
Look beyond its doors
The world can be a teacher
Many adventures are in store.
As long as you are hearing
Your education grows
That will lead to contributions
As you share the things you know.

3. Positive Ideas

GOAL you should be pursuing;
A DREAM your should be launching;
A PLAN you should be executing;
A PROJECT you should be starting;
A POSSIBILITY you should be exploring;
An OPPORTUNITY you should be grabbing;
An IDEA you should be working;
A PROBLEM you should be tackling;
A DECISION you should be making.
The greatest force in the world is a positive idea.

4. Don't Quit

When times are hard, you might stop for a bit,
But it's not over until the moment you quit.
On a river's bridge, failures are the planks;
Take one step at a time until you reach its banks.
Don't give up on your dreams; chase them instead;
You will find, one morning, as you wake up from bed,
That you are the person about whom you dreamed,
And you can reach great heights, impossible though it seemed.
When things go wrong and your back is to the wall,
Try to stand up; no more can you fall.
Life is full of ups and downs; take them in your stride.
You will discover your little star hidden inside.

5. Life Is Just Like A Road

Have you ever driven down a road?
Just to drive with no destination in mind.
The road seems to go on and on
With no stopping point.
Life is like that long road going on and on
not knowing when it's going to end.
But still you strive for another tomorrow
Hoping that in the long run
Everything will turn out alright
Just like the road though
It must come to an end.

6. Past, Present, Future

Our past we can't recapture. It's over and it's done.
No way to recover time; All those days are gone.
No amount of coloring painting with bright hue
can change the way things happened. No way to make it true.
No use fretting over Regretting bygone days No need to get
entangled In memory's purple haze.
Or caught up in unraveling
(or, of hoping we could do) things that didn't go the way
that we would want them to. The future is uncertain
No way for us to see,
the things that tomorrow's holding, for you or for me!
NOW is what's obtainable, just moments here to share.
The future comes so quickly – unseen but waiting there.
Seize the present moments. Grab all we can contain!
Our future are elusive. Our past we cannot chain!

7. The Stream of Life

Life… the essence of living
to breathe, to nourish, to create,
to exist on a common plain
and known no difference.
What if the world was this simple?
That the greatest life achievement,
The richest reward one could give
was to reap and bestow love.
The water falls from the skies, nourishes the land,
the living growth, creates a stream…creates life.
We bathe in its glory,
we shelter from its harshness, and sweeten our lips with delight.
We taste of love in the same manner
why do we not dance to the tune so simple and seek for nothing else?

8. Life Is Precious

The gracefulness of a butterfly, how gentle,
and fragile they seem.
Gently fluttering,
on a calm summers day, floating like,
a dream.
But sadly,
their time is over, Hardly before it's begun.
So enjoy
your special moments, like a butterfly,
in the sun.

9. Life

Life changes in every second
We never know what will happen We smile
We cry We win We lose
It turn around so quickly
That's why life is a subtly puzzle…
Strong wind or friendly breeze Hard rain and little drizzles
Burning rays of sun or cool moonlight
Add so much wonder to our life
We come We go
We arrived
And we departure from the world In this little we live
Amidst Birth and Death.

10. Never Give Up On Anything

It's Madness...

To hate all roses, because you got scratched by one thorn.

To give up all your dreams, because one did not come true.

To lose faith in prayers, because one was not answered.

To give up on your efforts, because one of them failed.

To condemn all your friends, because one of them betrayed.

Not to believe in love, because someone was unfaithful.

Remember that, another chance may come up.

A new friend, A new love, A new life.

Never give up on anything!

11. Hold Fast To Dreams

Hold fast your dreams,
they shelter you through lonely nights,
gently they become the pillow,
that puts destination in your sights.
Hold tight the memories, the heart ach
that burns, for the one who wins,
is the one who remembers and learns.
Nurture the moments, handle with care,
for destiny states,
for each heart there`s a pair.
Cast off the anger,
and its deep rooted seed, remember t'was anger ,
that caused your heart to bleed,
Snuggle each memory,
a warm blanket held tight, bringing
you vision, guidance, sunlight.
Push away despair, nurture the hope,
so impossible it seems,
but the only way out,
is to hold fast to dreams.

12. Follow Your Heart

I have my own dreams and my own desires.
Something for which I'm keen, want to set the world on fire.
But you are the one who is stopping me,
for who I really want to be.
What you said ain't my will
and I know I don't have such skills.
You tell me to have an aim,
I have it, still you blame.
Don't expect me to be the same,
you're just bothered about your fame.
I can't keep walking on your shoes,
my dreams are something I don't want to lose.
I just want to follow my heart,
but you're letting the dreams apart.

13. It Takes Courage

It takes strength to be firm,
It takes courage to be gentle.
It takes strength to conquer,
It takes courage to surrender.
It takes strength to be certain,
It takes courage to have doubt.
It takes strength to fit in,
It takes courage to stand out.
It takes strength to feel a friend's pain,
It takes courage to feel your own pain.
It takes strength to endure abuse,
It takes courage to stop it.
It takes strength to stand alone,
It takes courage to lean on another.
It takes strength to love,
It takes courage to be loved.
It takes strength to survive,
It takes courage to live.

14. I Follow My Dreams

I get laughed at, I get ignored,
I often feel trapped,
and I keep my thoughts stored.
People can be cruel and very mean,
but no matter what,
I follow my dreams.
Life has waves;
I know that.
But I stand brave
and just take the crap.
I may feel exhausted and totally creamed,
but no matter what,
I follow my dreams.
I know what I want, and I won't stop trying.
Quitting? I can't,
for now I'm flying.
It's impossible it seems, but no matter what,
I follow my dreams...
Life's battle don't always go
To the stronger and faster man,
But sooner or later the man who
wins Is the man who thinks he can.

15. Opportunity

With doubt and dismay you are smitten
You think there's no chance for you, son?
Why, the best books haven't been written
The best race hasn't been run,
The best score hasn't been made yet,
The best song hasn't been sung,
The best tune hasn't been played yet,
Cheer up, for the world is young!
No chance? Why the world is just eager
For things that you ought to create
Its store of true wealth is still meagre
Its needs are incessant and great,
It yearns for more power and beauty
More laughter and love and romance,
More loyalty, labor and duty,
No chance–why there's nothing but chance!
For the best verse hasn't been rhymed yet,
The best house hasn't been planned,
The highest peak hasn't been climbed yet,
The mightiest rivers aren't spanned,
Don't worry and fret, faint hearted,
The chances have just begun,

For the Best jobs haven't been started,
The Best work hasn't been done.

16. Life Still Has A Morning

If there is a future there is time for mending-
Time to see your troubles coming to an ending.
Life is never hopeless however great your sorrow- If you're looking forward to a new tomorrow.
If there is time for wishing then there is time for hoping-
When through doubt and darkness you are blindly groping.
Though the heart be heavy and hurt you may be feeling-
If there is time for praying there is time for healing.
So if through your window there is a new day breaking-
Thank God for the promise, though mind and soul be aching,
If with harvest over there is grain enough for gleaning-
There is a new tomorrow and life still has meaning.

17. Success

The road to success is not straight.
There is a curve called Failure,
A loop called Confusion,
Speed bumps called Friends,
Red lights called Enemies, and
Caution lights called Family.
But if you have a spare called Determination,
An engine called Perseverance,
Insurance called Faith, and
A driver called Jesus,
You will make it to a place called Success!!

18. Failure

Failure doesn't mean – "You are a failure,"
It means – You have not succeeded.
Failure doesn't mean – "You accomplished nothing,"
It means – You have learned something.
Failure doesn't mean – "You have been a fool," It means –
You had a lot of faith.
Failure doesn't mean – "You don't have it," It means –
You were willing to try.
Failure doesn't mean – "You are inferior," It means –
You are not perfect.
Failure doesn't mean – "You've wasted your life,"
It means – You have a reason to start afresh.
Failure doesn't mean – "You should give up," It means – "
You must try harder.
Failure doesn't mean – "You'll never make it," It means –
It will take a little longer.
Failure doesn't mean – "God has abandoned you,"
It means – God has a better way for you

19. Life Is A Gift

Life is a gift; a precious gift.
Precious than red diamond.
Beautiful than gold.
Life is a shining gift; it shines brighter than moissanite.
Life is a ticket; a free ticket.
The ticket is given to observe the beauty of creation.
It is not given to all, even though it's a free ticket.
It is given to only the chosen few,
Considered to be fortunate.
Life is a gift; a precious gift.
A gift wrapped with challenges.
You have to take up life's challenges,
In order to access its beauty.
The thickness of the wrapper varies.
The thicker your life's wrapper,
The difficult it gets to unwrap the gift.
This is why people face different difficult situations.
When you give your best,
And everything seems to go out of place,
Always remember that the difficulty you encounter,
Is simply because you are making progress.
Making an attempt to unwrap life's beauty.

If you refuse to open up the gift,
You will not have challenges to encounter.
You will not be faced with difficulty.
But your life will be meaningless.
You will live a life without a goal.
You will live a life without direction.
You will live a life without a dream.
You will live a life without ambition.
You will live a life without vision.
If you choose to run away from the wrapper of life; challenges
Know that you will never see the content (beauty) of your gift.
And your life will be worthless.
Is that what you want?
Life is a gift; a precious gift.
Anytime you are faced with challenges,
Learn to relax and stay positive.
It simply means that you are making progress.
You are getting closer to unwrapping life's beauty.
So, you don't have to be frustrated.
The challenges will surely pass away.
It's only a matter of time.
Don't give up on life. Don't do it!
The world waits to celebrate your life's beauty.
Millions of lives are waiting to celebrate with you,
For when you eventually unwrap life's beautiful gift.
Life is a ball; you have to kick it to score a goal.
The strength and force of your kick,

Will determine the motion of your life.
The direction of your kick,
Will determine your life's destination.
Therefore, learn how to live your life.
Learn to take responsibility for your life.
And ensure that you score a goal, if not goals.
Don't lose yourself in the struggle for life.
You don't need to struggle.
You just need to live.
You need to live your own life.
Learn to take a step at a time.
Learn to unwrap your gift with patient.
It doesn't matter if your friends are successful.
They were only faster than you to unwrap their gift.
And now they are enjoying the beauty of life.
It doesn't matter because you still have your life's gift.
Nobody can acquire your own life's beauty.
Life's gift is such that it is unique to its owner.
But one thing you must set your mind to do,
Is to ensure that you will unwrap your gift,
At your own pace and time.
And behold the beauty that awaits you in life.
Nobody can unwrap your gift on your behalf.
Only you can live the life you have.
Your life is for you alone to live.
Life is a gift; a precious gift.
It is a gift with a time frame.

It is a scheduled gift on life calendar,
With an expiring date programmed to it.
It has a time bomb with an unknown time reading.
Time defines life; make good use of your time to define your life.
You can't afford to waste time.
You can't afford to keep running away from challenges.
Face your life challenges, and unwrap life beauty,
When you still have the time to do so.
Life is a ticking time bomb,
And Death is the timekeeper.
Don't let the time bomb blow your life's beauty off.
And turn it to ashes.
Don't let your life's gift explode,
Before it is too late.
Don't live a wasted life,
So as not to live a life of regret.
Time cannot be purchased.
Use your time now,
Before it becomes irrelevant.

20. Life

Life is but a stopping place,
A pause in what's to be,
A resting place along the road,
to sweet eternity.
We all have different journeys,
Different paths along the way,
We all were meant to learn some things,
but never meant to stay...
Our destination is a place,
Far greater than we know.
For some the journey's quicker,
For some the journey's slow.
And when the journey finally ends,
We'll claim a great reward,
And find an everlasting peace,
Together with the lord.

21. Fear

Fear is loud and bossy.
She can be vicious at times.
And the worst of it is that
she often mingles truth with fiction.
But you must learn to challenge the stories she feeds you.
You get to be the boss of your thoughts.
You can learn to question whether or
not everything she tells you is truth,
whole truth,
and nothing but the truth. Since you have done
the work to deepen self-awareness
and self-compassion,
when she throws all your past failings in
your face you won't crumble
because you already know you are imperfect…
AND you are beautiful
and resilient and worthy of building a
thoughtfully crafted life.

22. Life Is A Strange

I ran into a stranger as he passed by.
"Oh, excuse me please" was my reply.
He said, "Please, excuse me too,
Wasn't even watching for you."
We were very polite, this stranger and I.
We went on our way and we said good-bye.
But at home a different story is told,
How we treat our loved ones, young and old.
Later that day, cooking the evening meal,
My daughter stood beside me very still.
When I turned, I nearly knocked her down.
"Move out of the way," I said with a frown.
She walked away, her little heart broken
at how harshly I had spoken.
While I lay awake in bed,
God's still small voice came to me and said,
"While dealing with a stranger, common courtesy you use,
But the children you love, you seem to abuse.
Look on the kitchen floor,
You'll find some flowers there by the door.
Those are the flowers she brought for you.
She picked them herself, pink, yellow and blue.

She stood quietly not to spoil the surprise,
And you never saw the tears in her eyes.
"By this time, I felt very small,
and now my tears began to fall.
I quietly went and knelt by her bed;
"Wake up, little girl, wake up," I said.
"Are these the flowers you picked for me?"
She smiled, "I found 'em, out by the tree.
I picked 'em, because they're pretty like you.
I knew you'd like'em, especially the blue.
I said, "Daughter, I'm sorry for the way I acted today;
I shouldn't have yelled at you that way."
She said, "Oh, Mom, that's okay.
I love you anyway."
I said, "Daughter, I love you too,
And I do like the flowers, especially the blue."

23. I Will Rise

I will rise
After every fall.
I will rise
And stand tall.

I will rise
Over the wall.
I will rise
Above them all.

Like the sun,
Which never dies.
Though sets every night,
Every day it does rise.

Like the ocean
Whose tides
Many times they are down,
But invariably they rise.

Like the trees,
From seeds they arise,

And heights great
They rise and rise.

After falling once,
Twice and thrice,
Again and again
I will rise and rise.

I will rise
After every fall.
After every fall
I will rise.

24. Life Is A Journey

Truly, life is a journey of joy and sorrow!
No guarantee for happiness in every tomorrow.
Always be prepare for both defeat and victory,
And rely on God's promise to keep you company.

25. Beauty Of Life

Like a little child without fear
I set forth on an unbeaten path
Upon a meadow bright and wild
Beauty of life is impressed
Dreams by the thousand blooms
I bravely danced among the flowers
Like butterfly floating bloom to bloom
Beauty of life is imbued
From a distance a stream is bidding
The menacing sound of gushing water
Turned to music as the birds sing
Beauty of life is induced

26. The Will To Win

If you want a thing bad enough
To go out and fight for it,
Work day and night for it,
Give up your time and your
peace and your sleep for it
If only desire of it
Makes you quite mad enough Never to tire of it,
Makes you hold all other things tawdry and cheap for it
If life seems all empty and useless without it
And all that you scheme and you dream is about it,
If gladly you'll sweat for it,
Fret for it, Plan for it,
Lose all your terror of God or man for it,
If you'll simply go after that thing that you want.
With all your capacity,
Strength and sagacity,
Faith, hope and confidence, stern pertinacity,
If neither cold poverty, famished and gaunt,
Nor sickness nor pain
Of body or brain
Can turn you away from the thing that you want,
If dogged and grim you besiege and beset it, You'll get it!

27. Promise Yourself

Promise yourself to be so strong that nothing can
disturb your peace of mind.
To talk health, happiness, and prosperity to
every person you meet.
To make all your friends feel like there is
something in them.
To look at the sunny side of everything and make your
optimism come true.
To think only of the best, to work only for the best,
and expect only the best.
To be just as enthusiastic about the success of others
as you are about your own.
To forget the mistakes of the past and press on the
greater achievements of the future.
To wear a cheerful countenance at all times and give
every living person you meet a smile.
To give so much time to the improvement of yourself
that you have no time to criticize others.
To be too large for worry, too noble for anger, and too
strong for fear, and to happy to permit the
presence of trouble.

28. Don't Quit

When things go wrong as they sometimes will;
When the road you're trudging seems all uphill;
When the funds are low, and the debts are high;
And you want to smile, but you have to sigh;
When care is pressing you down a bit
Rest if you must, but don't you quit.
Success is failure turned inside out;
The silver tint of the clouds of doubt;
And you can never tell how close you are;
It may be near when it seems afar.
So, stick to the fight when you're hardest hit –
It's when things go wrong that you mustn't quit.

29. When Is That Golden Moment?

When the scale tells me I've not gained a pound
When my glasses or phone or keys have been found,
When the cop pulls me over but spares me the ticket
When my ice cream cone drips and I get to lick it,
When I read the obituaries and don't know a soul,
When the car just ahead of me pays for my toll,
When my pants can fit without sucking my gut in
When I'm on the dance floor and a man asks to cut in,
When it's time for a movie and I get to choose it,
When I cut out the coupon and remember to use it.
Everyone understands the worth
Of a big celebration: a marriage, a birth
But moments of joy, too many to mention
Brighten each day, when we just pay attention.

30. Meaning of Life

The years have passed by
In the blink of an eye,
Moments of sadness
And joy have flown by.

People I loved
Have come and have gone,
But the world never stopped,
And we all carried on.

Life wasn't easy,
And the struggles were there,
Filled with times that it mattered,
Times I just didn't care.

I stood on my own,
And I still found my way,
Through some nights filled with tears,
And the dawn of new days.

And now with old age,
It's become very clear;

Things I once found important
Were not why I was here.

And how many things
That I managed to buy
Were never what made me
Feel better inside.

And the worries and fears
That plagued me each day,
In the end of it all,
Would just fade away.

But how much I reached out
To others when needed,
Would be the true measure
Of how I succeeded.

And how much I shared
Of my soul and my heart
Would ultimately be
What set me apart.

And what's really important,
Is my opinion of me,
And whether or not
I'm the best I can be.

And how much more kindness
And love I can show
Before the Lord tells me
It's my time to go.

31. Success

The road to success is not straight.
There is a curve called Failure,
A loop called Confusion,
Speed bumps called Friends,
Red lights called Enemies, and
Caution lights called Family.
But if you have a spare called Determination,
An engine called Perseverance,
Insurance called Faith, and
A driver called Jesus,
You will make it to a place called Success!!

32. What is success?

Happiness comes not from having much to live on
but having much to live for.
Success never resides in the world of weak wishes,
but in the palace of purposeful plans and prayerful persistence.

Pessimism achieves no success over persistence.
Temporary defeat never spells total failure;
one victory never assures permanent success.

A real success is one who makes
his mark in life without smearing others.
Excellence without effort is as futile as progress without preparation
Work can be our friend or foe, or joy or our woe.

Success, like happiness, is more than a destination -
it is a venture; more than an achievement - it is an attitude.
The greatest failure is the failure to try.
Alter your attitude and you will change your life.

Who seeks success, let him prepare.
Improvement is the son of discontent;

success is the offspring of preparation.
To emphasize the positive - the affirmative -
is to travel the high road of joy.
Success never resides in the world of weak wishes.
William Arthur Ward

33. Anyway

People are unreasonable, illogical, and self-centered.
Love them anyway!

If you do good, people will accuse you of selfish ulterior motives.
Do good anyway!

If you are successful, you will win false friends and true enemies.
Succeed anyway!

The good you do today, will be forgotten tomorrow.
Do good anyway!

Honesty and frankness make you vulnerable.
Be honest and frank anyway!

The biggest person with the biggest ideas can be shot down by the smallest people with the smallest minds;
Think big anyway!

People favor underdogs, but follow only top dogs.
Fight for underdogs anyway!

What you spend years building up may be destroyed overnight.
Build anyway!

People really need help, but will attack you if you help them.
Help them anyway!

Give the world the best you have and it may kick you in the teeth.
Give the world the best you've got anyway!
Give the world the best you've got.

34. Success Personified

To each morning the sun does shine
When all seems like a newborn time
To dwell in laughter so much
Is only the beginning for me to clutch.

I will go out to find
Intelligent people of like mind.
To suffer or endure
Of friends who but will not do.

To look upon the earth with glee
For all beauty is in me
To grasp the clouds way up high
There is more before I die.

May I go upon the street
Never ending on my feet
Seeking out the best in others
Always to find I have more brothers.

To make a part of the world
A better place you see.

For every one I must explore
To look upon them as no one before.

To seek out and help
Others is more than joy
To be valued and respected
In all my life reflected.

All of this as said before
Makes me want to reach out more
For it is a challenge for me to reach
This is success for all to preach.
"One life has breathed easier because you have lived"

35. A New Beginning

It's only the beginning now
...a pathway yet unknown,
At times the sound of other steps
...sometimes we walk alone.

The best beginnings of our lives
May sometimes end in sorrow,
But even on our darkest days
...the sun will shine tomorrow.

So we must do our very best
Whatever life may bring,
And look beyond the winter chill
...to smell the breath of spring.

Into each life will always come
A time to start anew,
A new beginning for each heart
...As fresh as morning dew.

Although the cares of life are great
And heads are bowed so low,

The storms of life will leave behind
...the wonder of a rainbow.

The years will never take away
Our chance to start anew,
It's only the beginning now
So dreams can still come true.

36. Trouble But Not Defeat

Underneath our feet we find
Those branches and thorns a grind.
Why is so life so mean
It is as if no other scene.
Through life, you know, you will find
We sometimes just close our minds.
Those solutions we so desperately want
All appear like yesterday's many tyrants.
But, do not trouble or be dismayed
There are good days on the way.
When you look beyond the norm
You'll find you need not conform.
Be bold, be happy, be confident
You are not meant to lament.
These things so sure today
Can vanish without delay.
So when trouble comes your way
Do not accept defeat and ruin your day
Move forward with a focused view
Stay positive in all you do.

37. Count Your Blessings

When you are feeling down
And all you can muster up is a frown
That is the time to stop
And count your blessings until you drop.
Focus on all of life's good
And you will find things work out as they should
Feeling sorry and just sitting around
It is a sure thing to bring you down.
Take some action, make a move
It doesn't matter if others approve
Nothing lasts forever
You will move past this if you endeavor!

38. Hidden Mystery

In the deepest depths of you and me
In the deepest depths of we
Lies the most beautiful jewel
Shining forth eternally
Within that precious jewel
Within that priceless piece of we
Lies a time beyond all time
Lies a place beyond all space
Within that sacred source of radiance
Lies a love beyond all love
Waiting
Waiting
Waiting
Ever so patiently
Waiting for you, waiting for me
Waiting patiently for all to see
The beauty that is you inside of me
The beauty that is me inside of thee
In the deepest depths of you and me
In the deepest depths of we
Lies the love and wisdom
Of all Eternity

39. Things You Can Control

Your Beliefs
Your attitude
Your thoughts
Your perspective
How honest you are
Who your friends are
What books you read
How often you exercise
The type of food you eat
How many risks you take
How you interpret the situation
How kind you are to others
How kind you are to yourself
How often you say "I love you."
How often you say "thank you."
How you express your feelings
Whether or not you ask for help
How often you practice gratitude
How many times you smile today
The amount of effort you put forth

How you spend / invest your money
How much time you spend worrying
How often you think about your past
Whether or not you judge other people
Whether or not you try again after a setback
How much you appreciate the things you have

40. Don't Disrespect Yourself

Why are you disrespecting yourself girl?
Don't you know you're a pearl?
You're a precious jewel,
Please honey, sweetie don't be no fool!
Your body is a temple before the Lord.
Don't mistreat it with harm.
Don't disrespect yourself!
Don't let no one slap you around and put you down.
Stand your ground and know who, and who's you are.
You were created by the creator.
Fearfully and Wonderfully made.
So don't disrespect your self
Put a stop and an end to this way of living.
Cease from the pain, get away from it all girl.
Don't let anyone disrespect you!
Don't you know you're a queen, a precious gem.
If not, take a look in the mirror
and see all the beauty which God have mad you to be.
So girl, sister, friend and all women around the world,
Don't disrespect yourself!

41. Don't Give Up

We wait for what we long for.
We long for what we need.
Impatience and anxiety
Give root to errant deed,
Which grows to yield but heartache,
The fruit that poisons trust,
And so to shadow we recede
And hope descends to dust.
But somehow from the ashes
The will to try again
Doth mend the heart
And forge the path
In search of that one friend
Who never will betray us,
Who never will go astray.
But fear still lurks upon the thought
While waiting for that day.
We'll simply stumble once again,
For we know not who to trust,
Thus thoughts becomes an enemy,
But conquer them we must.
For surely there is someone

Whether "Shining Knight" or "Bride."
Then all shall have been worth it,
Our "Last Hope" justified.

42. It Takes Courage

It takes strength to be firm,
It takes courage to be gentle.
It takes strength to conquer,
It takes courage to surrender.
It takes strength to be certain,
It takes courage to have doubt.
It takes strength to fit in,
It takes courage to stand out.
It takes strength to feel a friend's pain,
It takes courage to feel your own pain.
It takes strength to endure abuse,
It takes courage to stop it.
It takes strength to stand alone,
It takes courage to lean on another.
It takes strength to love,
It takes courage to be loved.
It takes strength to survive,
It takes courage to live.

43. You Cannot Change

You cannot change the world,
But you can present the world with one improved person –
Yourself.
You can go to work on yourself to make yourself
Into the kind of person you admire and respect.
You can become a role model and set a standard for others.
You can control and discipline yourself to resist acting
Or speaking in a negative way toward anyone for any reason.
You can insist upon always doing things the loving way,
Rather than the hurtful way.
By doing these things each day, you can continue on your journey
Toward becoming an exceptional human being.

44. Opportunity

With doubt and dismay you are smitten
You think there's no chance for you, son?
Why, the best books haven't been written
The best race hasn't been run,
The best score hasn't been made yet,
The best song hasn't been sung,
The best tune hasn't been played yet,
Cheer up, for the world is young!
No chance? Why the world is just eager
For things that you ought to create
Its store of true wealth is still meagre
Its needs are incessant and great,
It yearns for more power and beauty
More laughter and love and romance,
More loyalty, labor and duty,
No chance–why there's nothing but chance!
For the best verse hasn't been rhymed yet,
The best house hasn't been planned,
The highest peak hasn't been climbed yet,
The mightiest rivers aren't spanned,
Don't worry and fret, faint hearted,
The chances have just begun,

For the Best jobs haven't been started,
The Best work hasn't been done.

45. I'm Busy

I'm busy;
but not in the way
most people accept.
I'm busy calming my fear
and finding my courage.
I'm busy listening to my kids.
I'm busy getting in touch
with what is real.
I'm busy growing things and
connecting with the natural world.
I'm busy questioning my answers.
I'm busy being present in my life.

46. Keep Going by Kate Summers

When failures come – keep going
When you feel like giving up – keep going
When people mock your idea – keep going
When challenges you face – keep going
When mistakes are made, learn – but keep going
Because perseverance just keeps going!

47. Don't Quit

When things go wrong as they sometimes will;
When the road you're trudging seems all uphill;
When the funds are low, and the debts are high;
And you want to smile, but you have to sigh;
When care is pressing you down a bit
Rest if you must, but don't you quit.
Success is failure turned inside out;
The silver tint of the clouds of doubt;
And you can never tell how close you are;
It may be near when it seems afar.
So, stick to the fight when you're hardest hit –
It's when things go wrong that you mustn't quit.

48. Less Afraid

And then I realized
that to be
more alive
I had to
be less
afraid
so
I did it…
I lost my
fear
and gained
my whole life.

49. Embracing All

Light that lies deep inside of me
Come forth in all thy majesty
Show me thy gaze
Teach me thy ways
That I a better person may be
Darkness that lies deep inside of me
Come forth in all thy mystery
Show me thy gaze
Teach me thy ways
That I a better person may be
Love that lies deep inside of me
Come forth in all thy unity
Let me be thy gaze
Let me teach thy ways
That I a better person may be

50. The World That Awaits

The sun is shining,
On this amazing day,
Of new beginnings,
And farewells to say.

Our new road is paved,
With a new path in sight.
It's time to take it,
It feels quite right.

We will say farewell,
To all we've known.
The knowledge we will take with us
And no longer be attending class.

It's time to explore,
The world that awaits.
Allow yourself to,
Embrace your fate.

51. Tomorrow Holds A New Beginning

Time flies. Whether we like it or not, these past years of school
have caused us to grow up and become young adults,
ready to go out into the world.

We are all starting from the same place,
but we are all going in different directions.
We strive to obtain the goals we set for ourselves by
using what we've learned from the past.

Change happens, the excitement of our senior year is replaced
with cherished moments and memories of the past.
Different goals have been set after accomplishing previous ones.

Looking back in ten, twenty, thirty years,
there will be even more change we see in ourselves than we do now.
Living in the present allows us to appreciate the past.
Change allows us to see the progression of ourselves as
a generation of individuals: then and now.

52. Hope for Our New Beginning

We are excited for tomorrow
We will move forward without sorrow.
Our hopes and dreams we will see
Will be realized by us being all we can be.

What we have learned we shall give
We will do our best as we live
We start today as happy fellows
With hopes and dreams of a new tomorrow.

53. Seasons Of Life

Life brings many seasons
Change happens for a reason
So as one ending occurs
Look forward, open the doors.

A new beginning a time to do
All of the things you want to.
A time to look at yourself
And put away any doubts.

Believe that you can succeed
You have the potential to exceed
So take a deep breath and go
Don't be discouraged if it's slow.

A season ends and a new one begins
Don't lose your smile or your grin
With a positive attitude with you
You will find success in all you do.

54. Your Mission

If you cannot on the ocean
Sail among the swiftest fleet,
Rocking on the highest billows,
Laughing at the storms you meet;
You can stand among the sailors
Anchored yet within the bay;
You can lend a hand to help them
As they launch their boat away.

If you are too weak to journey
Up the mountain steep and high,
You can stand within the valley
While the multitudes go by;
You can chant in happy measure
As they slowly pass along;
Though they may forget the singer
They will not forget the song.

If you have not gold and silver
Ever ready to command;
If you cannot toward the needy,
Reach an ever-open hand;

You can visit the afflicted,
O'er the erring you can weep;
You can be a true disciple
Sitting at the Saviour's feet.

If you cannot in the harvest
Garner up the richest sheaves,
Many a grain both ripe and golden
Will the careless reapers leave;
Go and glean among the briers
Growing rank against the wall,
For it may be that their shadow
Hides the heaviest wheat of all.

If you cannot in the conflict
Prove yourself a soldier true,
If where fire and smoke are thickest
There's no work for you to do;
When the battle-field is silent
You can go with careful tread:
You can bear away the wounded,
You can cover up the dead.

If you cannot be the watchman,
Standing high on Zion's wall,
Pointing out the path to heaven,
Offering life and peace to all;

With your prayers and with your bounties
You can do what Heaven demands,
You can be like faithful Aaron,
Holding up the prophet's hands.

Do not, then, stand idly waiting
For some greater work to do;
Fortune is a lazy goddess--
She will never come to you.
Go and toil in any vineyard,
Do not fear to do or dare;
If you want a field of labor
You can find it anywhere.

55. The Last Day

To cherished hands of memory
We now must farewell speak,
But 'tis with sad and aching heart
That other climes we seek.
O'er the schoolroom and o'er campus
Our wistful gaze is cast,
Our days at school are numbered now
We've come now to the last.

But a new beginning is upon us
And forward will we march
With knowledge and a purpose
We will leave our mark.
We will always remember our days
And the friendships that we made
But we welcome the challenge of moving on
And working at our trade.

56. Great Endings And New Beginnings

On this day of all days,
Is a day of great endings.
The start of new beginnings,
Many wishes to be sent.

You will say goodbye to great friendships,
And mentors alike.
Start to make new friendships,
And see life with new sight.

Your journey awaits you,
You will take with you lessons learned.
And with each new day coming,
New lessons will be earned.

Although it's time to move on,
Life before will always be.
Your time spent learning
Will be a gift that was meant to be.

A new chapter is about to begin,

Congratulations on Your Accomplishment!

57. We're Graduating

Today is the day that we close our books,
And take a walk in an unknown place.
Many years we've spent in this building,
About to embark on a new rat race.

But now that our journey here is finished,
We will close our books to this page.
Our time here has been quite fulfilling,
Can't wait to start earning a wage!

Graduation is more than just saying,
Goodbye to a classroom of books.
It's leaving behind great friendships,
And mentors who always left you hooked.

So we say goodbye to all the great teachers,
And we'll miss you to all of our friends.
Hello to the new chapter that awaits us,
It's our turn to be making the trends.

58. Only The Beginning

You may feel graduation is the end
But let me tell you this friend
It is only the beginning
Your graduation is fitting
To start a new journey
And it won't be all easy
But the skills and lessons
Will help you thru the seasons.

Your life is ahead of you
Always do the best you can do
Don't let challenges stop you from
Being what you want to become.
Life will have its ups and downs
Along with smiles and frowns.
But as you journey on the road ahead
Follow your heart, be not led.

59. Life Has A Way

Life has a way of changing our days
From graduation to death
Oh it changes in many ways
So live each day and be thankful.

Life is full of challenges to
But then there is excitement
And always lots to do
So look forward each day.

Strive to do your best
Never stop learning
It will keep you ahead of the rest
Always improving every day.

With every ending comes a new beginning
Keep your attitude positive
And you will find yourself singing
Through each chapter of your life

60. Life May Be Tough

Life may be tough
Things will get rough
There will be bad days
Life may seem like a haze
But through it all
Always, always stand tall
Giving up is not an option
Never turn your back and run
Through good times and bad
Through happy times and sad
As long as you keep moving
You'll never stop growing

61. Stop Worrying About

Stop worrying about
What everyone else is doing
Just keep your focus
On where you want to be going
Believe in moving forward
No matter how slow
Change, takes a lot of time
Progress, even more so

62. So You Failed, That Ain't a Bit Deal

So you failed, that ain't a bit deal
Stop the excuses, stop taking names
Toughen up, get back on your feet
Jordan missed 9000 shots, lost 300 games
Part and parcel of life, is failure
Don't run away, keep trying again
Ruthless, how much life may seem
In the end, the win is worth the pain

63. So What If You Made

So what if you made
A mistake, life doesn't stop
So what, if you had a setback
You can still get back on top
Failure is temporary
And by the way, so is success
Nothing else matters
When all you seek is progress

64. A Student

A Student
What does it mean to be one
Books and exams
Is that all there is to it hun?
No, replied the wise man
For, with a smile, he said
We are all students
Till the time we're dead
Metaphorical, may this story be
But his words can't be truer
Nothing can stop you in life
As long as you are a learner

65. Education Has A Value

Education has a value
That sometimes cannot be quantified
If you ever doubt your journey
Look within, instead of looking outside
Deep inside your heart
Lie answers to all questions of life
No one else but you and your goals
Will keep you afloat in strife
Keep working hard
Focus on your long term goal
Its not the excuses that count
But the fire in your soul

66. Education Is Like Life

Education is like life
And vice versa too
It's a long journey, that
Can make or break you
Shortcuts to success
There are none
It's always hard work
That pays in the long run

67. Homework might seem

Homework might seem
Boring and of little value
But put your heart into it
It'll teach you things new
Homework, ain't homework
Unless you look at it so
It's an opportunity to learn
An opportunity to grow

68. Being A Student

Being a student
Ain't that easy
But hey, it was
Never meant to be
Stop the excuses
They ain't setting you free
Just focus and be
The best you can be

69. Study Hard Today

Study hard today
For a better tomorrow
Learn and absorb
Let curiosity glow
Life is a long battle
Sometimes a tad too cruel
In the end, it pays off
To winners in school

70. A Lesson from History

Everything's easy after it's done;
Every battle's a "cinch" that's won;
Every problem is clear that's solved--
The earth was round when it _revolved!_
But Washington stood amid grave doubt
With enemy forces camped about;
He could not know how he would fare
Till _after_ he'd crossed the Delaware.
Though the river was full of ice
He did not think about it twice,
But started across in the dead of night,
The enemy waiting to open the fight.
Likely feeling pretty blue,
Being human, same as you,
But he was brave amid despair,
And Washington crossed the Delaware!
So when you're with trouble beset,
And your spirits are soaking wet,
When all the sky with clouds is black,
Don't lie down upon your back
And look at _them_. Just do the thing;
Though you are choked, still try to sing.

If times are dark, believe them fair,
And you will cross the Delaware!

71. A Time To Believe

To believe is to know that
every day is a new beginning.
Is to trust that miracles happen,
and dreams really do come true.
To believe is to see angels
dancing among the clouds,
To know the wonder of a stardust sky
and the wisdom of the man in the moon.
To believe is to know the value of a nurturing heart,
The innocence of a child's eyes
and the beauty of an aging hand,
for it is through their teachings we learn to love.
To believe is to find the strength
and courage that lies within us
When it's time to pick up
the pieces and begin again.
To believe is to know
we are not alone,
That life is a gift
and this is our time to cherish it.
To believe is to know
that wonderful surprises are just

waiting to happen,
And all our hopes and dreams are within reach.
If only we believe.

72. Can You Sing a Song?

Can you sing a song to greet the sun,
Can you cheerily tackle the work to be done,
Can you vision it finished when only begun,
Can you sing a song?
Can you sing a song when the day's half through,
When even the thought of the rest wearies you,
With so little done and so much to do,
Can you sing a song?
Can you sing a song at the close of the day,
When weary and tired, the work's put away,
With the joy that it's done the best of the pay,
Can you sing a song?

73. It Takes Courage

It takes strength to be firm,
It takes courage to be gentle.
It takes strength to conquer,
It takes courage to surrender.
It takes strength to be certain,
It takes courage to have doubt.
It takes strength to fit in,
It takes courage to stand out.
It takes strength to feel a friend's pain,
It takes courage to feel your own pain.
It takes strength to endure abuse,
It takes courage to stop it.
It takes strength to stand alone,
It takes courage to lean on another.
It takes strength to love,
It takes courage to be loved.
It takes strength to survive,
It takes courage to live.

74. Letting Go

To let go doesn't mean to stop caring;
It means I can't do it for someone else.
To let go is not to cut myself off...
It's the realization that I can't control another...
To let go is not to enable,
but to allow learning from natural consequences.
To let go is to admit powerlessness,
which means the outcome is not in my hands.
To let go is not to try and change or blame another,
I can only change myself.
To let go is not to care for, but to care about.
To let go is not to fix, but to be supportive.
To let go is not to judge,
but to allow another to be a human being.
To let go is not to be in the middle arranging all the outcomes,
but to allow others to affect their own outcomes.
To let go is not to be protective,
It is to permit another to face reality.
To let go is not to deny, but to accept.
To let go is not to nag, scold, or argue,
but to search out my own shortcomings and correct them.
To let go is not to adjust everything to my desires,

but to take each day as it comes and cherish the moment.
To let go is not to criticize and regulate anyone,
but to try to become what I dream I can be.
To let go is not to regret the past,
but to grow and live for the future.
To let go is to fear less and love more.

75. Life Still Has A Meaning

If there is a future there is time for mending-
Time to see your troubles coming to an ending.
Life is never hopeless however great your sorrow-
If you're looking forward to a new tomorrow.
If there is time for wishing then there is time for hoping-
When through doubt and darkness you are blindly groping.
Though the heart be heavy and hurt you may be feeling-
If there is time for praying there is time for healing.
So if through your window there is a new day breaking-
Thank God for the promise, though mind and soul be aching,
If with harvest over there is grain enough for gleaning-
There is a new tomorrow and life still has meaning.

76. Just One

One song can spark a moment,
One flower can wake the dream.
One tree can start a forest,
One bird can herald spring.
One smile begins a friendship,
One handclasp lifts a soul.
One star can guide a ship at sea,
One word can frame the goal
One vote can change a nation,
One sunbeam lights a room
One candle wipes out darkness,
One laugh will conquer gloom.
One step must start each journey.
One word must start each prayer.
One hope will raise our spirits,
One touch can show you care.
One voice can speak with wisdom,
One heart can know what's true,
One life can make a difference,
You see, it's up to you!

77. TheMan Who Thinks He Can

If you think you are beaten, you are
If you think you dare not, you don't,
If you like to win, but you think you can't
It is almost certain you won't.
If you think you'll lose, you're lost
For out of the world we find,
Success begins with a fellow's will
It's all in the state of mind.
If you think you are outclassed, you are
You've got to think high to rise,
You've got to be sure of yourself before
You can ever win a prize.
Life's battles don't always go
To the stronger or faster man,
But soon or late the man who wins
Is the man WHO THINKS HE CAN!

78. Life Is A Gift

Life is a gift we're given each and every day.
Dream about tomorrow, but live for today.
To live a little, you've got to love a whole lot.
Love turns the ordinary into the extraordinary.
Life's a journey always worth taking.
Take time to smell the roses, daffodils and lilacs.
Count blessings like children count stars.
The secret of a happy life isn't buried in a treasure chest . . . it lies within your heart.
It's the little moments that make life big.
So don't wait. Make memories today and celebrate your life!

79. Befo You Act

Before you act, listen.
Before you read, think.
Before you spend, earn.
Before you criticize, wait.
Before you pray, forgive.
Before you quit, try.

80. Education : The Key To Life

Education
the light of our life
A gift of academic rife
Education
the key to a bright and rewarding future
A glue that joins our dreams like a suture
Education
A path to divine success
A smooth drive to our greatness
Education
gives our thinking a different appearance
And helps drive away all our ignorance
Education
It leads us to the path of prosperity
And gives our tomorrow a sounding security
Education
the process of teaching and learning
Which will help us in our future earning
Education
shaping our true character is the motto

Leading to a successful life it is the major factor
Education
The progressive discovery of our true self
And exploitation of the potentials of oneself
Education
a better safeguard of liberty than a standing army
A life boat that see us through our days of stormy
Education
A torch of academic brilliance
And backbone of inner resilience
Education
the key to unlock the golden door of freedom
And stage our rise to stardom
Education
A life sustaining material
Without it we can't lead a life which is congenial
Education
not all about bookish knowledge
But it is also about practical knowledge
Education
makes a person stand up on his on toes
And helps a person to fight with all his foes
Education
A fundamental foundation
For any country state or nation
Education
A thick line between right and wrong

A ladder that takes us to the height where we belong
Education
Mother of all profession
That helps acquires all our possession
Education Is our right
For in it our future is bright.

"Why are we so afraid to fall in love?
Is it the hurt, the heartbreak, or not being enough?
Why are we so afraid to even try?
To take a risk, to jump to soar, to fly?
But in this lifetime I can't seem to say
I'll find someone for me, I'll find someone who'll stay".

www.ingramcontent.com/pod-product-compliance
Ingram Content Group UK Ltd.
Pitfield, Milton Keynes, MK11 3LW, UK
UKHW040010200726
13854UKWH00001B/125

9 798886 297782